Royal Bird – Peacock

CALENDAR 2024

and

Stories
for
Children

Elena Pankey

978-1-952907-78-4

CONTENTS

***

The ancient Greeks believed that the flesh of the peacock never decayed, even after death, and so it became a symbol of immortality.

Early Christians adopted the symbolism and the peacock thus became an emblem of the Resurrection and the eternal life of Christ.

***

Royal Bird – Peacock
Calendar 2024

Stories for Children

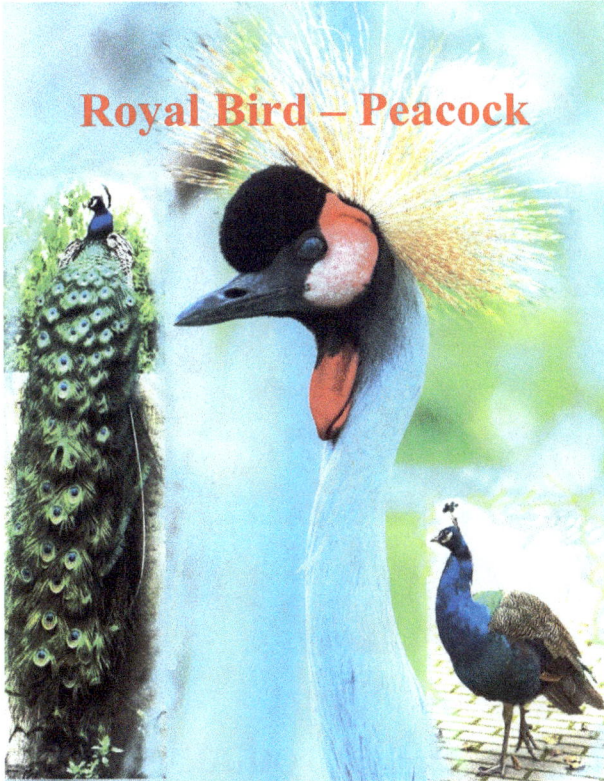

Royal Bird – Peacock

Elena Pankey
***

ISBN: 9781952907784

3

***

It dances today, my heart, like a peacock it dances, it dances. It sports a mosaic of passions like a peacock's tail. It soars to the sky with delight, it quests. Oh, wildly, it dances today, my heart, like a peacock it dances (Rabindranath Tagore).

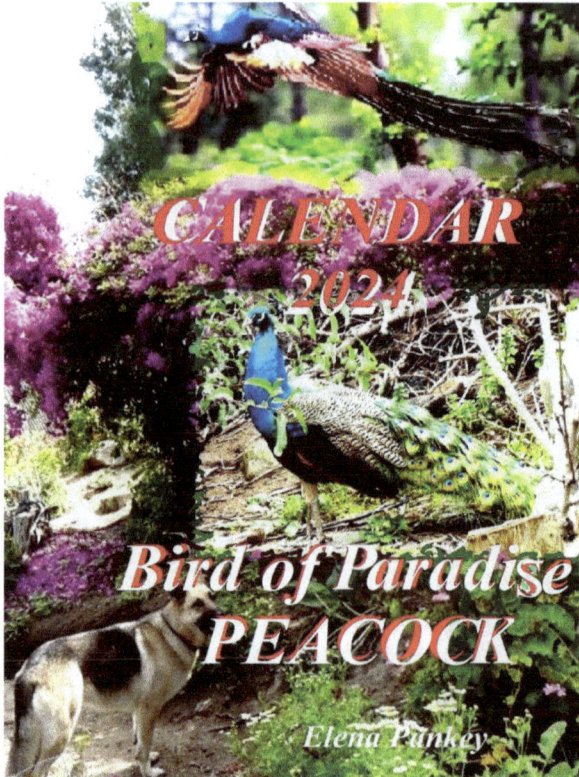

***

Introduction

Month by month Calendar 2024 "Royal Bird-Peacock" has beautiful photos of this unique bird. Also, it has some interesting information and smart proverbs about this "Paradise Bird", as people called it.

It is useful to know about unusual naturel creates and good to share this story with your children.

This Calendar is a good gift for anyone and any time of the year. Enjoy

***

December 2023

DECEMBER 2023

SUN	MON	TUE	WED	THU	FRI	SAT
					1	2
3	4	5	6	7	8	9
10	11	12	13	14	15	16
17	18	19	20	21	22	23
24	25	26	27	28	29	30
31						

"Genius and virtue are to be more often found clothed in gray than in peacock bright."

***

What does a peacock symbolize?

While representing different meanings to different cultures, the peacock, with its unique beauty, makes it a handy symbol for power, strength, confidence, and even divinity, something with which most monarchs throughout history have wanted to be associated.

***

5

All 2024

2024

January
S	M	T	W	T	F	S
	1	2	3	4	5	6
7	8	9	10	11	12	13
14	15	16	17	18	19	20
21	22	23	24	25	26	27
28	29	30	31			

February
S	M	T	W	T	F	S
				1	2	3
4	5	6	7	8	9	10
11	12	13	14	15	16	17
18	19	20	21	22	23	24
25	26	27	28	29		

March
S	M	T	W	T	F	S
					1	2
3	4	5	6	7	8	9
10	11	12	13	14	15	16
17	18	19	20	21	22	23
24	25	26	27	28	29	30
31						

April
S	M	T	W	T	F	S
	1	2	3	4	5	6
7	8	9	10	11	12	13
14	15	16	17	18	19	20
21	22	23	24	25	26	27
28	29	30				

May
S	M	T	W	T	F	S
			1	2	3	4
5	6	7	8	9	10	11
12	13	14	15	16	17	18
19	20	21	22	23	24	25
26	27	28	29	30	31	

June
S	M	T	W	T	F	S
						1
2	3	4	5	6	7	8
9	10	11	12	13	14	15
16	17	18	19	20	21	22
23	24	25	26	27	28	29
30						

July
S	M	T	W	T	F	S
	1	2	3	4	5	6
7	8	9	10	11	12	13
14	15	16	17	18	19	20
21	22	23	24	25	26	27
28	29	30	31			

August
S	M	T	W	T	F	S
				1	2	3
4	5	6	7	8	9	10
11	12	13	14	15	16	17
18	19	20	21	22	23	24
25	26	27	28	29	30	31

September
S	M	T	W	T	F	S
1	2	3	4	5	6	7
8	9	10	11	12	13	14
15	16	17	18	19	20	21
22	23	24	25	26	27	28
29	30					

October
S	M	T	W	T	F	S
		1	2	3	4	5
6	7	8	9	10	11	12
13	14	15	16	17	18	19
20	21	22	23	24	25	26
27	28	29	30	31		

November
S	M	T	W	T	F	S
					1	2
3	4	5	6	7	8	9
10	11	12	13	14	15	16
17	18	19	20	21	22	23
24	25	26	27	28	29	30

December
S	M	T	W	T	F	S
1	2	3	4	5	6	7
8	9	10	11	12	13	14
15	16	17	18	19	20	21
22	23	24	25	26	27	28
29	30	31				

Dream tonight of peacock tails, Diamond fields and spouter whales. Ills are many, blessing few, But dreams tonight will shelter you.
***

The phrases "a flash of turquoise", "violet fringed with golden amber", "dark glowing eyes", "eyes that are always open" and "tail that has to blink" describe the beauty of a peacock.
***

***

"A peacock has too little in its head, too much in its tail."

January 2024

JANUARY 2024

SUN	MON	TUE	WED	THU	FRI	SAT
	1	2	3	4	5	6
7	8	9	10	11	12	13
14	15	16	17	18	19	20
21	22	23	24	25	26	27
28	29	30	31			

Actually, the name peacock applies only to the male.

***

"She is a peacock in everything but beauty."

***

The pride of the peacock is the glory of God.

February 2024

FEBRUARY 2024

SUN	MON	TUE	WED	THU	FRI	SAT
				1	2	3
4	5	6	7	8	9	10
11	12	13	14	15	16	17
18	19	20	21	22	23	24
25	26	27	28	29		

If someone is as proud as a peacock, they are extremely proud.

***

"Sparrows who emulate peacocks are likely to break a thigh."

***

March 2024

MARCH 2024

SUN	MON	TUE	WED	THU	FRI	SAT
					1	2
3	4	5	6	7	8	9
10	11	12	13	14	15	16
17	18	19	20	21	22	23
24	25	26	27	28	29	30
31						

"A peacock has too little in its head, too much in its tail."

***

"If thou be wise, view the peacock's feathers with his feet, and weigh
thy best parts with thy imperfections."

***

April 2024

APRIL 2024

SUN	MON	TUE	WED	THU	FRI	SAT
	1	2	3	4	5	6
7	8	9	10	11	12	13
14	15	16	17	18	19	20
21	22	23	24	25	26	27
28	29	30				

"Sparrows who emulate peacocks are likely to break a thigh."

***

Remember that the most beautiful things in the world are the most useless; peacocks and lilies for instance.

***

May 2024

MAY 2024

SUN	MON	TUE	WED	THU	FRI	SAT
			1	2	3	4
5	6	7	8	9	10	11
12	13	14	15	16	17	18
19	20	21	22	23	24	25
26	27	28	29	30	31	

"She is a peacock in everything but beauty."

***

"Be like a tree, bloom like a flower, sing like a bird, and dance like a peacock."

June 2024

JUNE 2024

SUN	MON	TUE	WED	THU	FRI	SAT
						1
2	3	4	5	6	7	8
9	10	11	12	13	14	15
16	17	18	19	20	21	22
23	24	25	26	27	28	29
30						

The pride of the peacock is the glory of God.

***

"Whenever I can put a fresh, clean suit on, I'm like a peacock.

***

July 2024

JULY 2024

SUN	MON	TUE	WED	THU	FRI	SAT
	1	2	3	4	5	6
7	8	9	10	11	12	13
14	15	16	17	18	19	20
21	22	23	24	25	26	27
28	29	30	31			

Remember that the most beautiful things in the world are the most useless; peacocks and lilies for instance.

***

The phrases "a flash of turquoise", "violet fringed with golden amber", "dark glowing eyes", "eyes that are always open" and "tail that has to blink" describe the beauty of a peacock.

August 2024

AUGUST 2024

SUN	MON	TUE	WED	THU	FRI	SAT
				1	2	3
4	5	6	7	8	9	10
11	12	13	14	15	16	17
18	19	20	21	22	23	24
25	26	27	28	29	30	31

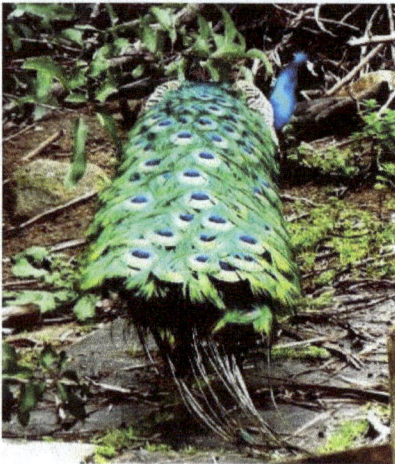

Proud as a peacock" is a saying that is used to mean a vain or self-centered person.

The phrase comes from the plumage of the male peafowl (females are peahens).

When a male is courting, he spreads his tail feathers, sometimes five feet in length, out in a fan pattern to attract a female.

***

"Be like a tree, bloom like a flower, sing like a bird, and dance like a peacock."

***

To Paradise, the Arabs say, Satan could never find the way
Until the peacock led him in (Charles Godfrey Leland)
***

14

September 2024

SEPTEMBER 2024

SUN	MON	TUE	WED	THU	FRI	SAT
1	2	3	4	5	6	7
8	9	10	11	12	13	14
15	16	17	18	19	20	21
22	23	24	25	26	27	28
29	30					

The phrases "a flash of turquoise", "violet fringed with golden amber", "dark glowing eyes", "eyes that are always open" and "tail that has to blink" describe the beauty of a peacock.

***

"Whenever I can put a fresh, clean suit on, I'm like a peacock.

***

People are crying up the rich and variegated plumage of the peacock, and he is himself blushing at the sight of his ugly feet (Saadi).

***

15

October 2024

OCTOBER 2024

SUN	MON	TUE	WED	THU	FRI	SAT
		1	2	3	4	5
6	7	8	9	10	11	12
13	14	15	16	17	18	19
20	21	22	23	24	25	26
27	28	29	30	31		

It dances today, my heart, like a peacock it dances, it dances. It sports a mosaic of passions like a peacock's tail, It soars to the sky with delight, it quests, Oh wildly, it dances today, my heart, like a peacock it dances (Rabindranath Tagore).

***

Be motivated like the falcon, hunt gloriously. Be magnificent as the leopard, fight to win. Spend less time with nightingales and peacocks. One is all talk, the other only color (Rumi).

16

November 2024

NOVEMBER 2024

SUN	MON	TUE	WED	THU	FRI	SAT
					1	2
3	4	5	6	7	8	9
10	11	12	13	14	15	16
17	18	19	20	21	22	23
24	25	26	27	28	29	30

Be motivated like the falcon, hunt gloriously. Be magnificent as the leopard, fight to win. Spend less time with nightingales and peacocks. One is all talk, the other only color (Rumi).

***

Proud as a peacock" is a saying that is used to mean a vain or self-cen tered person. The phrase comes from the plumage of the male peafowl (females are peahens). When a male is courting, he spreads his tail feathers, sometimes five feet in length, out in a fan pattern to attract a female.

***

17

December 2024

DECEMBER 2024

SUN	MON	TUE	WED	THU	FRI	SAT
1	2	3	4	5	6	7
8	9	10	11	12	13	14
15	16	17	18	19	20	21
22	23	24	25	26	27	28
29	30	31				

People are crying up the rich and variegated plumage of the peacock, and he is himself blushing at the sight of his ugly feet (Saadi).

The sun fades like the spreading Of a peacock's tail, as though twilight Might be read as a warning to those desperate For easy solutions (John Ashbery)

***

The sun fades like the spreading Of a peacock's tail, as though twilight Might be read as a warning to those desperate For easy solutions (John Ashbery)

18

Royal Bird – Peacock

"The tale is a lie, but there is a hint in it, a lesson for good fellows." Many Russian fairy tales ended with such a saying. Old grandmother sometimes told this proverb her little granddaughter, trying to teach her the wisdom of ancient beliefs. Do you believe in miracles?

One morning in our garden there was a piercing, as if calling someone, the cry of a large bird. We have never heard such a strange and loud cry. The windows of the southern part of the house overlooked the garden. At night, they were closed with protective metal blinds, keeping house warm. And in the morning we opened them to the bright sun that burst into the kitchen, downstairs office and living room. Glancing out in that huge kitchen window, we were struck by a strange vision of a blue bird strutting about the garden as if it already owned it.

To our deepest surprise, it was the most beautiful peacock, with a very long tail feathers. These rainbow-colored feathers had special markings typical of this species of peacock, and they were looking like eyes.

Suddenly, seeing that I was approaching him, the peacock, apparently, wanted to make the best impression and show off his amazing beauty. He lifted his tail up, opened it like a fan, and shouted his greeting three times. He achieved a striking effect, and we froze in surprise, not daring to frighten him away.

How could such a "bird of paradise" get into the garden of our ranch which was locating on a high hill, far from people and civilization. In addition, the garden was surrounded by a metal fence.

The peacock solemnly and slowly rejoiced at the vast space where he suddenly found himself, and pecked at something on the ground. Then, he settled himself comfortably under a bush, rested a little, and again began to walk around the garden, shouting loudly and calling for at least someone to keep him company. Peacocks do not like to live alone, on their own, they become sad. And then they shout a lot and loudly, calling their friends to join them.

Some time ago, we noticed that someone was wandering around the house and in the garden at night, spoiling our flowers, bushes and trees. One day, these bandits poisoned our devoted dog who courageously defended the garden from their invasion. His old friend, the impressionable and affectionate shepherd Sonya, witnessed the death of her old friend at the hands of bandits. After that she stopped barking altogether, being afraid to attract the attention of some strangers on the ranch.

In that same year, when we lost our courageous dog, and in order to escape the bitterness of that loss, we adopted a new puppy. But young Tuzik did not know any fear, and barked loudly, sensing enemies somewhere nearby, stealing avocados or other fruits. Fearing for my devoted dogs, I did not want to leave them alone in the fenced yard for the night. Old, quiet Sonya and young Tuzik slept in their own rooms in the house.

With the advent of the Peacock in the garden, I wanted to learn more about these amazing birds. They used to live in the Pacific Islands, India, and Australia. According to legend, Dutch pioneers saw the birds and named them "Birds of Paradise".

This was the reason why the "Birds of Paradise" (or in some Russian tales it was called as "Firebirds") were present only in the stories of sailors who admired the bright plumage of birds.

Beautiful birds from legends attracted a lot of attention of most royalties and they loved to have them in their parks. The peacock embodies a symbol of shining glory, immortality, greatness and incorruptibility. But also, they were a symbol of pride and vanity. In the ancient cultures of India and Iran, the magnificent peacock's tail became a symbol of the all-seeing Sun and eternal cosmic cycles.

In addition, I learned that these birds have very sensitive sleep. And no criminal will be able to sneak into the garden unnoticed without waking the "Firebird". The bird will start screaming loudly, calling for everyone to help. So, a Peacock might become an excellent defender for the garden.

In addition, this handsome Peacock could be not just a decoration of our garden. All day he consumed all the harmful insects that were in abundance in the garden, lizards and even snakes. He had strong, sharp toenails and could at least repel someone's aggression or lightly attack those who interfered with him.

Our Peacock often came very close to the house, and settled comfortably under a canopy where our old dog once lived. There he sat for a long time, looking into the distance, remembering his former domestic life in the narrow and cramped space of the cage. Now he happily and loudly called his girlfriends to join him in his new life in paradise. Soon it became clear to us that someone had brought him to us at night in a plastic bag, which we found by the trees. Someone was, like us, at first struck by the beauty of this royal bird and wanted to own it, without studying its features.

And the frequent heartbreaking cries of male peacocks during the mating season cause quite natural displeasure of neighbors. Peacocks scream very sharply, and it is especially unpleasant to hear their "singing" in the dark.

Peacocks need a lot of space, and suffer when living in domestic cages or in a small area of the backyard of some little town. Apparently, the neighbors of the former frivolous owners of the peacock tired of his loud cries, and began to complain about the violation of their peace. And, wanting to get rid of this rash purchase, the previous owners of the Peacock dropped the bird while he was sleeping, at our ranch.

It was not only interesting to watch that beautiful bird (a gift from the sky), thinking about perishability of being beautiful. The peacock, as it were, prompted thoughts about the need to shine, to show oneself from the best side, and to please with your own beauty the one who lived nearby.

But again, one inconvenience nevertheless soon began to interfere with our quiet life. It was March and Peacock loudly screamed a lot. It was clear that he was very lonely, even in a beautiful and large garden.

Suddenly, somehow, dogs jumped into the garden, and Tuzik rushed after the Peacock. But the bird quickly took off, and, having flown a little, sat down on a spreading oak at the bottom of the road, not far from the garden. He sat there and menacingly (as it seemed to him) trumpeted very loudly, exactly like an elephant, in the same low voice. The peacock was apparently frightened, and wanted to drive the young dog away from the oak.

Old dog Sonya stood nearby silently surprised at all this energetic and unusual activity in her quiet garden. The loud barking of the two-year-old Tuzik at a defenseless bird sitting high in a tree seemed especially unnecessary to her. After looking a little more at all this unnecessary fuss, she left. And I had to take Tuzik to the front yard, away from the garden.

And Peacock, it seemed, disappeared for the whole next day. And we didn't hear his three-fold call to his friends to join his new paradisiacal life in the vast garden. But suddenly, a day later, a miracle happened again. We saw and heard Peacock again. He bustled along the lower road, loudly declaring his indispensable desire to return to the safety of the upper garden.

But Tuzik, possessed by the thirst for hunting, again rushed after the bird, trying to grab it with his sharp teeth. And the Peacock nevertheless flew up again to the same oak tree in the orchard and outside of the fenced garden. And from his safe height, he sedately observed what we would do next, and whether he should again descend into the unexpectedly dangerous, and full of dogs, garden.

We left, leaving Peacock alone. And suddenly in the evening, we heard the piercingly loud, but short, cry of the Peacock resounding through the neighborhood of the ranch. He desperately called for some help when a flock of coyotes (jackals) made their way to the oak tree, under which the wounded Peacock sat.

The next day, the dogs and I went to the oak tree and dogs became agitated, running around it, sniffing the ground. The most beautiful bluish-green feathers from the tail of a magical bird were laying everywhere under the oak tree. This is all that remains of the handsome Peacock.

Feeling guilty, I brought these beautiful feathers home and placed them in a vase. In the corner of a tall refrigerator, they stood like a memory, or like an urn with the ashes of a dead person dear to you, whom you did not care about while he was alive ...

But these dead feathers in the corner were only a dull reflection of that unearthly beauty that the peacock demonstrated in the garden. The feeling of guilt torments the conscience, as it "eats" a person.

Now I am very sorry that we did not save this beautiful bird, which somehow miraculously ended up in our garden. He carelessly and importantly walked there, periodically spreading his wonderful tail like a fan, demonstrating his unearthly beauty, and shouting about the futility of a dull existence, where there is no concern for beauty.

Maybe one morning this bird of paradise will again miraculously appear in the garden, waking us up with a special loud cry calling for a friend...

I would like to believe in miracles or work miracles myself...

So, now we went on a journey to find the bird of Paradise…

***

***

Poem

Beneath the sky of blue the golden city stands with crystal-clear lucent gates and with a star ablaze. The garden lies within it blossoms far and wide. The beasts of stunning beauty are roaming inside.

There is a lion with a fiery-yellow mane, and the blue calf has eyes so deep and bright. There is the golden eagle from the heavens, whose eternal gaze's so unforgettable…

And from that sky of blue the star is shining through. This star is yours, oh angel mine. It always shined for you.

Who loved is beloved. Who giveth light is blessed. So go after the light of guiding star into this awesome land.

The fiery lion will meet you at the gate; and the blue calf with eyes so deep and bright. And the golden eagle from the heavens, whose eternal gaze's so unforgettable…

***

***

23

The Peacock

His loud sharp call seems to come from nowhere. Then, a flash of turquoise is in the papal tree (*Sacred fig*). The slender neck arched away from you as he descends, and as he darts away, a glimpse of the very end of his tail. I was told that you have to sit in the veranda and read a book, preferably one of your favorites with great concentration. The moment you begin to live inside the book a blue shadow will fall over you.

The wind will change direction. The steady hum of bees in the bushes nearby will stop. The cat will awaken and stretch. Something has broken your attention. And if you look up in time you might see the peacock turning away as he gathers his tail to shut those dark glowing eyes, violet fringed with golden amber. It is the tail that has to blink for eyes that are always open.

***

***

I Saw a Peacock

(The 400 Year-Old Nonsense Poem)
I Saw a Peacock, with a fiery tail,
I saw a Blazing Comet, drop down hail,
I saw a Cloud, with Ivy circled round,
I saw a sturdy Oak, creep on the ground,
I saw a Pismire, swallow up a Whale,
I saw a raging Sea, brim full of Ale,
I saw a Venice Glass, Sixteen foot deep,
I saw a well, full of men's tears that weep,
I saw their eyes, all in a flame of fire,
I saw a House, as big as the Moon and higher,
I saw the Sun, even in the midst of night,
I saw the man that saw this wondrous sight.
(A 'Pismire', by the way, is an old word for an ant.)
***

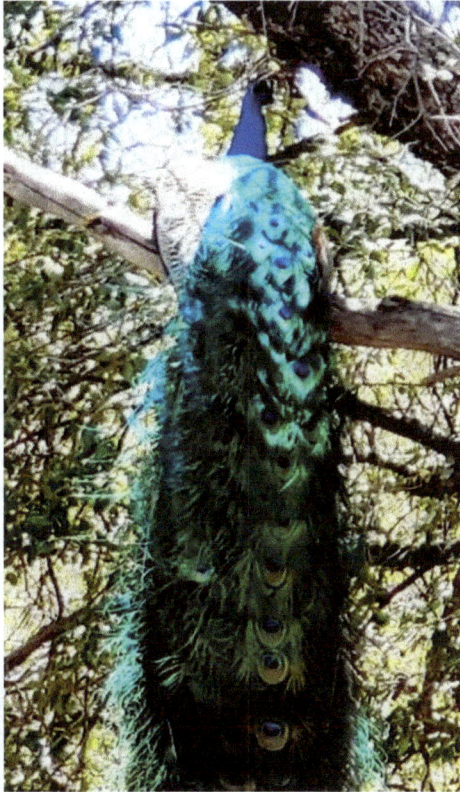

King Solomon and the Peacock (Ahmad Shawqi)

I heard that once upon a time a peacock came to King Solomon, heading a delegation of feathery folks. He was ostensibly displaying its plumes, showing off its flashy garments. Alternately, revealing and concealing its bright feathers. He said to the King: "I have a case I wish to present before you. I think it is time, your majesty, you looked into it. That's why, my Lord, I came here at your doorsteps. Am I not the meadows incarnate; with all their blossoms and sparkling lights? Haven't I gathered in my person every form of beauty, every shade and hue of color?

Here I am, the Master of all birds at your door! Must I be left without what I most eagerly desire? When I am of noble lineage and decent descent?

Alas, here I am, deprived of a melodious voice! I have never been able to enchant the hearts with my sweet tuneful strains, Nor I entertain the ears with my songs. Behold, the littlest of birds is capable of inflaming the passions of lovers. Yea, even kings sway when a singing bird warbles, swaying on its branch."

King Solomon answered, saying: "Thus has it been ordained! Great is God's wisdom, wonderful are His handiwork. Indeed, you are self-conceited! Nor are you content with what God has created. You call yourself the king of birds, yet are lacking in wisdom and understanding. Well, dear peacock, had you a beautiful voice, You would be even haughtier, Moreover, you would not deign to talk to anyone"…

***

26

About Author

Elena Pankey has more than 45 years of job experience in different areas. Elena is an Argentine Tango Master, and people called her "Twinkles Feet", "Queen of Tango," "Tango Icon".

She is the author of many fun books on different subjects, including fun fairy tales, children's books, about dogs and cats, about Argentine Tango dancing, art, and adventures. While living in CA, she continues to travel the world, teaching, dancing and writing.

***

Rights Reserved

***

New Books

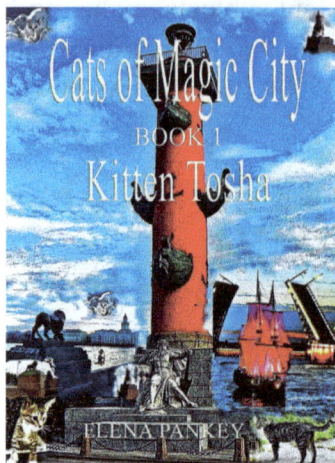

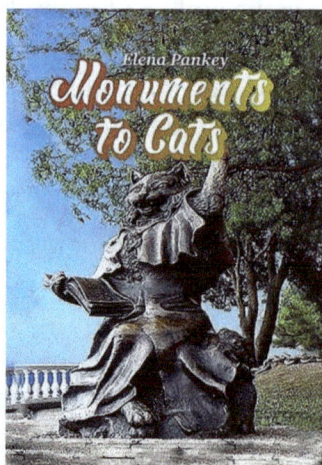

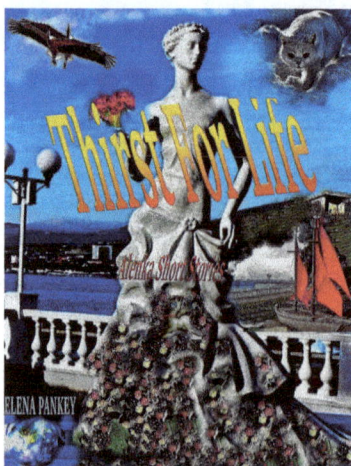

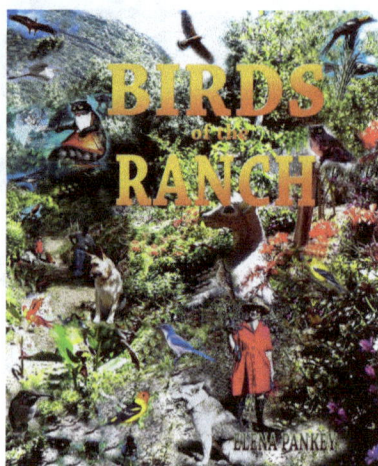

www.ingramcontent.com/pod-product-compliance
Lightning Source LLC
Chambersburg PA
CBHW070032030426
42335CB00017B/2405